DK READERS

BEGINNING
1
TO READ

STAR WARS

THE CLONE WARS

Ahsoka in Action!

Written by
Jon Richards

Ahsoka Tano is a Togruta.
She has orange skin, white face
markings, and long, blue and
white striped head-tails.

A Note to Parents

DK READERS is a compelling program for beginning readers, designed in conjunction with leading literacy experts, including Dr. Linda Gambrell, Distinguished Professor of Education at Clemson University. Dr. Gambrell has served as President of the National Reading Conference, the College Reading Association, and the International Reading Association.

Beautiful illustrations and superb full-color photographs combine with engaging, easy-to-read stories to offer a fresh approach to each subject in the series. Each DK READER is guaranteed to capture a child's interest while developing his or her reading skills, general knowledge, and love of reading.

The five levels of DK READERS are aimed at different reading abilities, enabling you to choose the books that are exactly right for your child:

Pre-level 1: Learning to read
Level 1: Beginning to read
Level 2: Beginning to read alone
Level 3: Reading alone
Level 4: Proficient readers

The "normal" age at which a child begins to read can be anywhere from three to eight years old. Adult participation through the lower levels is very helpful for providing encouragement, discussing storylines, and sounding out unfamiliar words.

No matter which level you select, you can be sure that you are helping your child learn to read, then read to learn!

LONDON, NEW YORK, MUNICH,
MELBOURNE, and DELHI

Editor Pamela Afram
Project Art Editor Clive Savage
Managing Editor Laura Gilbert
Design Manager Maxine Pedliham
Art Director Ron Stobbart
Publisher Simon Beecroft
Publishing Director Alex Allan
Pre-Production Producer Rebecca Fallowfield
Senior Producer Shabana Shakir
Jacket Designer Satvir Sihota

Designed and edited by Tall Tree Ltd
Designer Malcolm Parchment
Editor Jon Richards

Reading Consultant Linda B. Gambrell, Ph.D.

For Lucasfilm
Executive Editor Jonathan W. Rinzler
Art Director Troy Alders
Keeper of the Holocron Leland Chee
Director of Publishing Carol Roeder

First American Edition, 2013
10 9 8 7 6 5 4 3 2 1
Published in the United States by DK Publishing
375 Hudson Street, New York, New York 10014

DK books are available at special discounts when purchased in bulk
for sales promotions, premiums, fund-raising, or educational use.
For details, contact:
DK Publishing Special Markets
375 Hudson Street, New York, New York 10014
SpecialSales@dk.com

A catalog record for this book is available
from the Library of Congress.

ISBN: 978-1-4654-0583-8 (paperback)
ISBN: 978-1-4654-0584-5 (hardback)

Color reproduction by Alta Image
Printed and bound in China by L.Rex

Discover more at
www.dk.com
www.starwars.com

Jedi

Ahsoka is training to be a Jedi.
Being a Jedi is exciting, but it
can also be dangerous!
Hold on tight, Ahsoka!

Ahsoka goes on many
missions with the other Jedi.
The other Jedi include her
friends Anakin Skywalker,
Yoda, and Luminara Unduli.

Asajj Ventress

A Jedi's job is to protect people
from the evil Sith, such as the
wicked Asajj Ventress.
The Sith lead a huge army of
battle droids.

Ahsoka Tano   Luminara Unduli

Sith

Someone who is training to be
a Jedi is called a Padawan.
A Padawan learns to use a
special sword called a lightsaber.

Anakin teaches Ahsoka how
to fight with a lightsaber.
Ahsoka is so good that she can
use two lightsabers at once!

Ahsoka and Anakin have
many adventures and fight
in many battles together.
Hold on to that rope, Ahsoka.
Don't look down!

Ahsoka learns to use the Force. It lets her leap great distances or control the minds of others. She can even use it to push her enemies away without even touching them!

Ahsoka can jump very far and leap around quickly.
This makes her a good fighter and very hard to beat.

She can even defeat an army
of battle droids easily.
Ahsoka leaps toward the
droids, flashing her lightsabers.

Sometimes, Ahsoka has to fly her starfighter into space to fight enemy ships. Ahsoka is an excellent pilot.

Droid fighters
are no match for
her fantastic
flying skills.

starfighter

Jedi missions take Ahsoka to
many different planets.
She has ridden a speeder bike
into battle on the planet Kiros.
She also swam in the sea on the
planet of Mon Cala.

Not every Jedi mission involves fighting against the Sith. Sometimes Ahsoka and Anakin have to hide or wear a disguise.

Be careful, Ahsoka!
You don't want your enemies
to spot you!

Not everyone
Ahsoka meets
is friendly.

One of her greatest enemies
is the evil Ventress.
Watch out for that lightsaber!

Ahsoka also fights against
General Grievous.

cyborg

He is a cyborg who leads the evil battle droid army.
He has four arms and can fight with a lightsaber in each hand.

As well as fighting enemies, Ahsoka has to protect people. These include politicians, such as Senator Padmé Amidala, or the stinky Huttlet called Rotta.

Rotta

senator

Ahsoka may need help
from her friends.
When she is captured by
Trandoshans, Chewbacca
the Wookiee helps Ahsoka
to defeat the hunters.

No matter how hard Ahsoka fights, there are always people to be rescued and enemies to battle and defeat.

A Jedi's work is never done, so Ahsoka is always ready for action!

Glossary

cyborg
Someone who is part robot and part human.

Jedi
Someone who uses the Force for good.

senator
A person who is part of the government.

Sith
Someone who uses the Force for evil.

starfighter
A small spacecraft that is used in battles.